# Mr. Topaz is Left in Charge

## By Tracey Jude
## Illustrated by Jake Murray

*Mr. Topaz is Left in Charge*
c/o Tracey Jude
PO Box 10036
Fort Wayne, IN  46850-0036

E-mail: traceyjude@msn.com
Phone: 260.710.2637

Include name, address and phone number in the correspondence. Orders will be invoiced to include shipping and applicable tax.

ISBN  978-0-9800711-4-6

Printed in the United States of America.

This book is dedicated to the honor and memory of:

Sergeant Major (SGM) Jeffrey A. McLochlin
1961 - 2006

One who clearly knew his purpose in life
and bravely answered the call to serve.

Photo used with permission. To learn more about SGM McLochlin, go to Memory-Of. com.

## July 16, 2006

For the sole purpose of fulfilling the rhyme, 'Sarge' was first introduced in **Mr. Topaz is Left in Charge.** This came about after my son's struggle to creatively illustrate the original character, 'Marge'. While 'Sarge' could have been either gender, Jake determined that Mr. Topaz's owner would be a man. The design of the character was derived entirely from his own imagination.

At the time of this character's illustration, I learned the tragic news of SGM McLochlin's combat death on July 5. A gymnasium full of family and friends mourn the loss of their son, husband, father, brother, soldier and friend. For nearly 20 years, freedom was granted to millions of Americans, including the illustrator who never heard of the man but appears to be drawing some likeness of my classmate, the younger Jeff McLochlin.

While I am blessed to have known Jeff, I was ever more blessed to know he was simply around. Our divergent interests separated us socially, yet the peace shared in his hallway greetings conveyed all would be well. I wonder if my classmate ever knew the effect of his welcoming, calm demeanor and confident stride, for it is only now, looking back, that I realize how myopic I was to his gift. It is fitting that I remember Jeff, the comforting classmate and future peace keeper, after having just completed the story of a cat who unexpectedly finds a greater purpose to his own existence.

I find the correlation of this book and the reality of the loss most difficult to ignore. I feel compelled to do more than simply publish and market this book. Perhaps a greater purpose has just been revealed. I find myself stunned to learn of a greater purpose for this book while Mr. Topaz learns the very same lesson about himself in this story.


## August 22, 2007

On the 21st anniversary of SGM McLochlin's enlistment in the United States Army, I receive the final and complete illustration of **Mr. Topaz is Left in Charge.** It is only now, while reviewing the record of his service, that I notice this additional coincidence in the passing of time. SGM McLochlin is missed as much today as ever. Our freedom rings on as much today as ever due to the great sacrifice and service of this one man and others who have stepped up to answer the call to serve in their own, unique way.

God bless SGM Jeffrey A. McLochlin, God bless our troops, God bless America, and God, bless the world.
   - Tracey Jude, MT-BC

 This book belongs to:

_____

Who helps others by:

1 _____

2 _____

3 _____

Mr. Topaz lives with Sarge.

Left in charge meant left alone
to be the one to answer the phone.

He went outside only to find
that left in charge meant left behind.

He shook, shook until he tired out,
for whatever was inside would not fall out.

He tapped on the bottom,
he tapped on the top.

...until he heard the word

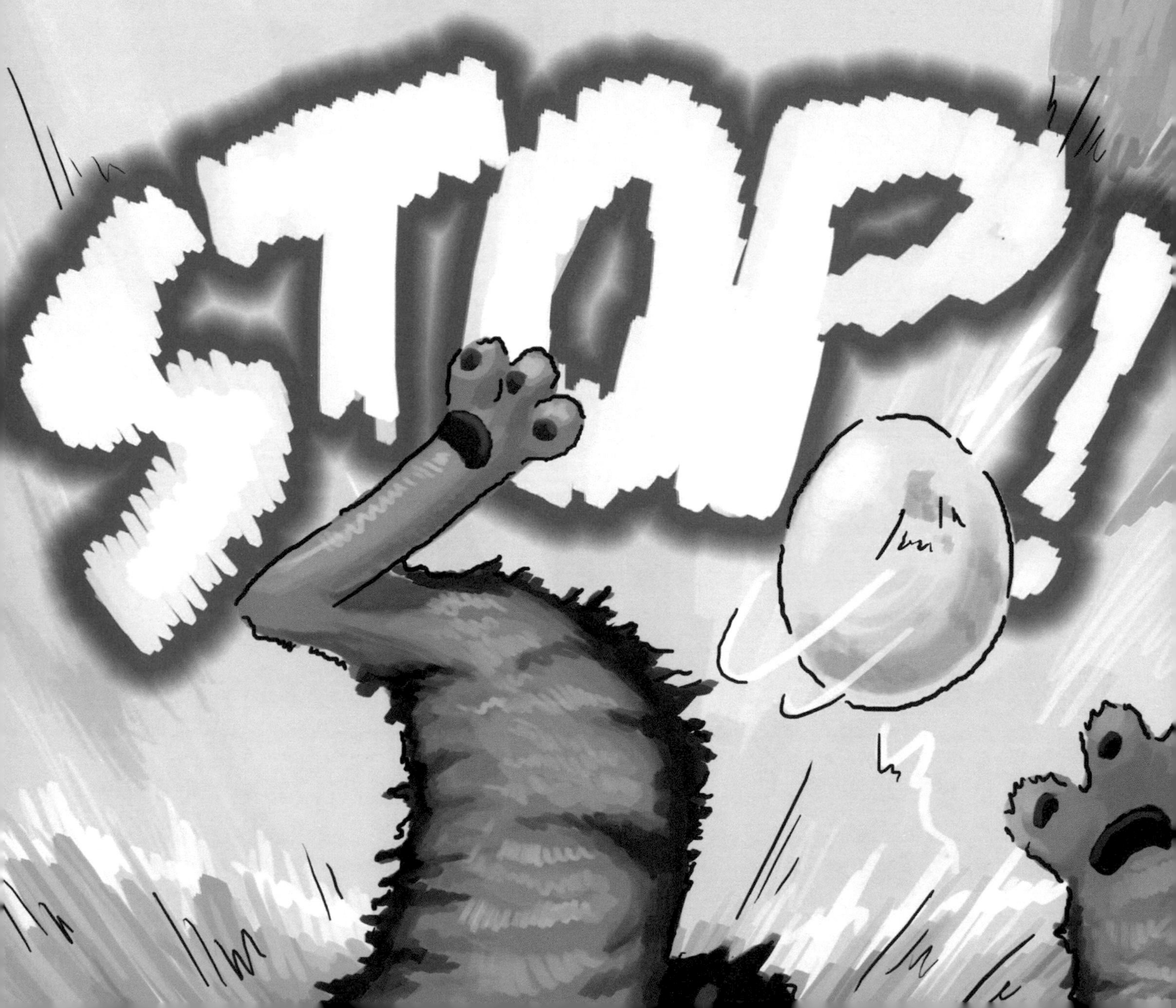

But Sarge didn't see a broken gourd.
Sarge saw what he was looking for.

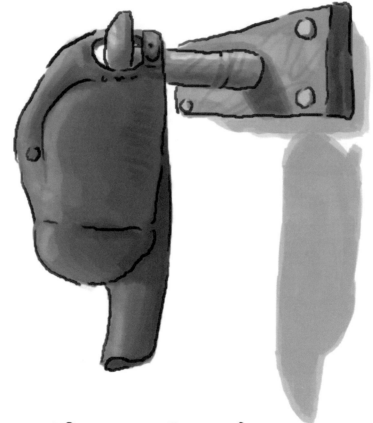

The End

# A Purpose to Ponder . . .

Mr. Topaz's job was:

   a) to answer the phone

   b) to fix the gourd

   c) to find the lost shaker egg

# Answer: C

Mr. Topaz doesn't answer the phone, and he didn't fix the gourd, but he did find the shaker egg.

Sometimes we don't know we are doing a more important job until we discover it by surprise.

# More Pondering about Purpose . . .

A shaker egg is used to make music. That is its job.
How do you think Sarge felt when he lost his musical instrument?
How did he feel when Mr. Topaz found it?

Mr. Topaz thought he was fixing a gourd, but in truth, he was making music.
How can you use music when you feel bored, sad, or alone? What is your favorite song?

How did Mr. Topaz feel at the beginning of the story?
Did he feel the same way throughout the story?
How did he make himself useful when he was in charge?
How would you feel being left in charge? What would you do?

Have you ever been surprised to find that your job was more important than
you thought it was? What job might you do to help others? Go back to the
the front of the book and read what you wrote on this page:

This book belongs to:
_____

Who helps others by:

1 _____
2 _____
3 _____

Add more lines as you discover more jobs that you can do!

Mr. Topaz, 2006

# About the Author

Tracey Jude is a wife and mother of 3 grown children and a board certified music therapist in private practice. She is a member of the American Music Therapy Association and gives private music lessons from her home.

The photograph above shows the author reading the anger-management book, *Mr. Topaz Takes a Walk* to a local preschool.

*Mr. Topaz is Left in Charge* is the second story of the series.

Tracey with client, 2006

9176749R0

Made in the USA
Charleston, SC
17 August 2011